ONCE UPON A TIME FROM THE IRON CURTAIN

A Great Escape

Joe Pataki

Copyright © 2024 (Joe Pataki)
All rights reserved worldwide.

No part of the book may be copied or changed in any format, sold, or used in a way other than what is outlined in this book, under any circumstances, without the prior written permission of the publisher.

Publisher: Author (Joe Pataki)
Edited by First Editing

Author: Joe Pataki
Title: Once Upon a Time from the Iron Curtain
Genre: Nonfiction / Memoir

Paperback ISBN: 978-0-646-89934-3

Acknowledgement

This book is a testimony about faith and trust in God. I am dedicated to all who experience trauma and mental health issues such as PTSD being forced to live their normal life and take refuge in other countries because of political aggression of the communist regime.

I thank God for this extraordinary experience of achieving a bachelor's degree, and for being with me every step of my life from the beginning of my Christian life, which started 35 years ago, and I thank all who helped me in my journey of faith, may God bless them all.

I dedicated this book to my wife Alina, who shoulder-to-shoulder shared with me for the last 46 years, struggles, joy, and happiness.

To my son and my daughter who gave me joy and happiness as they are growing up from their childhood to the teenage years, and later to their achievement as young adults. Thank you for the joy you give me as a father, for all the Disney cartoons that I wouldn't have any clue about if I did not watch with you. Thank you for being such great kids.

Special thanks to my University teachers, Rev. Doc. Dean O, Dr John Griffiths, Dr Darrel Potts, and all other teachers who helped me to grow from a caterpillar to a butterfly in the knowledge of Scripture and reshape my personality.

As a Chaplain, I would like to thank to Doctor (General) Ralf Estherby Director of Chaplaincy Australia and Jeff Marshal (Chaplaincy SA) who made me put into practice and understand cross-cultural leadership /Pastoral care.

Once upon a time from the Iron Curtain - A great escape

On February 21, 1989, the full moon spread its light over the stern and frozen agricultural soil not far from the village of Valcani, Romania. Two shadows crawled from the house at the edge of the village around 11:00 p.m. towards the fence that separated the border of the two countries. The distance was approximately 700 metres. Joe and Vic were ex-military, with bodies fit enough to endure crawling on the rugged winter land, but their morale was very low because they feared what could happen when they reached the fence. However, Vic did not find any difficulty in fast crawling, "probably because he is 30 kilograms lighter than me," meditating Joe on his weight.

Their commando suits were homemade by Vic, and their faces were covered with black shoe cream as if they'd dropped down from a chimney. The idea was to make them invisible, or so they thought, but the full moon fully exposed them to 100 metres of radium. Fortunately, it was unlikely there were sentinels in the tower and no patrols in the area around at this time. Finally, they reached the fence, nearly in delirium from the pain of crawling such a long distance.

Joe, who considered himself the leader of this dangerous adventure, asked Vic to hold the lower wire of the fence so he could cut it with pliers. Unfortunately, it was so cold that Vic did not have a proper grip on the wire, and when Joe produced the cutters, a harsh metallic noise filled the air. They both froze in panic, stopped breathing, and listened for a while to the silence of that strange night.

"See the rocket wire?" asked Vic.

"Yes," replied Joe I'm going to slide down into the channel; help with my movements." With his face down, Joe slowly slid into the channel. He felt the cold water penetrate through his pants, and the sensation of the cold, soft mud deviated his mind to his old training days. "This mud is weird. "It's like it never ends." He could not feel the bottom yet; it was already over his chest, just like in the movies when people fell into deep sinkholes. He started to panic and raised his head, touching the wire.

Vic had been taken by surprise, but his hands were already under the wire, and his response was fast, protecting the movement of the wire and pushing Joe's head down. They looked at the rocket grenade pin that had nearly come off, and they did not move for a while. Joe continued to slide until he touched the hard soil, and he then supervised Vic sliding into the channel more effortlessly.

The channel was designed to make enough noise to reach the dog's ears, trained to bark when they heard movement. So, they both lifted their feet very slowly, step by step, in that concentrated mud. It seemed to take an eternity to cross the four-metre channel. They crawled to the top of the edge and spotted the six-metre sentinel tower, but no one was on duty at night. They observed the two little bridges, each about a hundred metres from where they were.

"How lucky, we are right in the middle", observed Vic, and they started running.

They sprinted like they were in a running competition, propelled by fear and madness. When they stepped on the four metres of sand, Vic realised they had crossed no-man's-land. He pointed this out to Joe, whose adrenaline made it hard for him to recognise anything. "Look, we just passed the border,

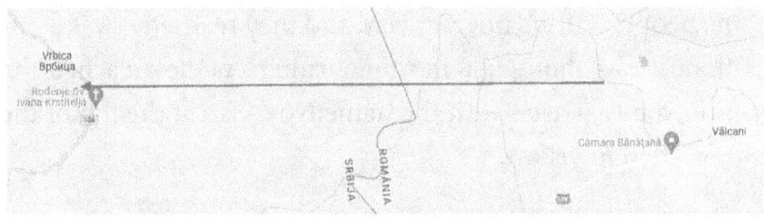

"We're in Yugoslavia, Joe". They could not believe it; they felt a freedom they had never experienced before. Then, after walking and catching their breath for a few moments, a lovely fontanel, something from the Middle Ages, appeared in front of them, like an affirmation of another world. They took off the black overcoats they wore over their regular clothing. Joe removed his army knife and threw everything into the fontanel. Then, from the wood bucket sitting on top, they washed their faces, adjusted the little bags on their shoulders and headed to the village in front of them.

"Did you intend to use that?" said Vic, referring to the army knife.

"I'm not sure; it doesn't matter now", said Joe, irritated by the idea.

They walked into a relatively quiet, strange village, like a chase table, with all streets divided in a perfect square. The village's name was Virbica, which was directly opposite the border with Valcani. They chose the middle road; it was so quiet that they heard their shoes on the pavement and saw the vapour from their breath. Suddenly, a car's noise passed, and they followed the sound to the end of the village, where a highway lined up in front of them.

They were walking on the left side of the road when they saw some people waiting not far away, and they realised it was a bus station. It was about 4:30 in the morning. As they reached the station, a bus arrived with the name Novi-Sad at the top of the bus, written in yellow.

They followed the people onto the bus, going for the seats at the back. A conductor came to sell tickets, and Joe gave him one hundred dinars, so he would not need to ask about the price. He feared it would cost more, but the conductor gave him the rest of the 20 dinars.

They could not see much from the bus in the darkness and probably did not even care to see something. Their only thoughts when the adrenaline started to dissolve, were questioning themselves if they were a free people and how far they would get before someone discovered them **Crossing Yugoslavia**

The rule in Yugoslavia was that if someone crossed their border illegally should report it to the police immediately or risk being deported back to where they came from. The country had an immigration camp at Bania Covalacha, where people waited for visa approval to the USA, Canada and Australia. The waiting time for a visa could take two years; in the meantime, people could work at the brick factory for nearly nothing; however, they did have a faster visa application. It was better than being sold back to Romania for a wagon of salt!

The only way to avoid this situation is not to be caught by the police and, second, to reach Austria or Italy. Joe got all this information from a Serbian guy, a salesman from whom Joe used to buy cigarettes, Vegeta powder, watches or shoe runners. But to reach the second border, they needed to travel over Croatia and Slovenia, which were part of Yugoslavia then. It seemed an unrealistic dream because only a low percentage of Romanian migrants could reach that area of Austria without being caught; however, they had to try this option.

At about six in the morning, the bus arrived in Novi-Sad. A beautiful station appeared with a different world and culture when they stepped off the bus. The boys entered the large building, and Joe approached the desk and posed as a Romanian tourist, asking if they could change some money. The woman told them to wait and brought the manager, who enquired how much he wanted to change. Joe said he would like to change about 20,000 Lei. The manager and the female clerk looked at each other with surprising smiles, and after a few moments, the deal was on. Joe received about 500,000 Serbian dinars and 100 Deutsche Marks. They could not believe their eyes about this honest transaction, and after a quick thanks, they left the place looking over their shoulders to see if someone was following them.

A young taxi driver waiting for customers outside the building invited them on his taxi. When they asked him which would be the best way to reach Zagreb, the guy pointed towards an office where they could buy tickets for the express bus to Zagreb. So they went to the front window, and Joe asked for two tickets to Zagreb. The woman pointed to a bus that would leave in half an hour and had only one stop on the trip. That was convenient because they 'didn't want to be seen hanging around. So they entered the bus and waited anxiously for departure, and the bus took them on their longest journey towards freedom.

The Shadow of Communism

Joe remembered how Tina, his sister, begged him to take her husband Vic on this mad escape. At first, he did not even want to consider this idea, but his wife, Alina, convinced him that going alone on such a journey was not good. He accepted the proposal, but also because Joe had a soft heart and had shown compassion for his sister because of her unjust and bitter life at a young age.

With his head on the bus window, Joe was overwhelmed with memories and a world much like a black-and-white movie. It was a time of communist corruption where poor people lived in block apartments. There was low morale, no religion or hope, but some mysticism probably produced by the high alcoholism. It started in 1985 when the Government lost all its economic and political credentials with Western countries, and Ceaushescu distanced himself from Russia's domination. As a paranoic madman, he brought back the Stalinist era of intellectual persecution, and everyone who made negative comments against his "ideologic" communist party was locked up in prison. People could get in trouble even for a simple joke.

It was hard to find decent food because he exported everything to demonstrate he could achieve zero international financial debt and did not need to depend on the West or East for support.

Rationed food distribution was only for the communist elite and the security forces. They had their private shops, and if you knew someone who knew someone, you might be lucky to buy some food for the family. However, people who lived in the country had a higher standard of living because of their farms.

For Joe, this world was ideal. As an electrician with knowledge of automation and system control, he had access to the food industry, trading one kilo of butter for theatre tickets provided by the director himself. He changed cacciatore salami from the meat industry, around 80 Lei ($US 20), for petrol, another expensive commodity. Eventually, he became corrupt, and money poised him with desire and immoral feelings. His cousin, a superior officer, invited him to the elite security club, where there were parties once a month and plenty of drinks. He got access to the underground private mini cinema, watching the latest five-star movies, and in winter, he dressed like a mobster, wearing an Alain-Delon long sheep leather jacket, leather boots, and the finest black astrakhan hat; the only thing that he was missing was a stick with a gold handle!

Slovenia

After the bus crossed the Serbian state, they arrived in Slovenia and stopped at a large petrol station for fuel. The driver said they could get food from the buffet inside, advising that the bus would leave in 30 minutes. Joe bought two burgers, their first delicious food after nearly two days, and watched the modern cars travel past on the smoothest road they had ever seen from the window. At the beginning of the trip, they decided not to talk, so no one could hear them talking in the Romanian language.

But Vic could not help but whisper to Joe, "I never seen such a smooth road. How is this possible?"

Joe explains that Slovenia had the same ideology of communism or socialism but a different culture and a civilisation close to Western society open to modernism and democracy.

The boys learned from a Croatian woman that both Slovenians and Croatian people hated Serb's domination. At that time, they knew nothing about their culture and relationship with those nations and probably didn't care much about this. The only thing that mattered to them was to avoid the police.

The bus left the station on time and headed to Zagreb, the capital of Slovenia. Watching through the windows, Joe's memories of the recent events from his country started emerging from the darkness.

Six days ago.
The Beginning of the End

Deep in his soul, Joe was sick of his pagan, miserable, sinful life. He had reached rock bottom morally and ethically and done some awful, disgusting things that made him ashamed. Drugged on those destructive behaviours by an entourage of friends and relatives from parties involving unlimited alcohol, he tried to find a way to escape. The worst was his cousin, an officer in the security forces, who influenced Joe to drink heavily and have fun with women. The only way to change his life was to start over and escape from that large south Transylvanian town and his darkness, seeking a new beginning in a new world.

He dreamt of crossing Yugoslavia and going to Austria, so he started planning the escape by studying a map and calculating the route. He thought spirituality might help, so he started praying, reading the Bible, and even visiting the ' 'town's Orthodox Church.

Nothing seemed to happen until he received a letter from the army "inviting" him to be reenlisted in the Army Technical Unit (ATU), which had participated in constructing

Ceaușescu Palace. Joe was shocked and devastated. He tried to pull strings with every prestigious person he knew to intervene and stop his enrolment. However, the colonel in charge of recruitment was under pressure to find people for his delicate and secret mission. So, the countdown for his planned escape begins.

Day 1

The meeting room was full of young people who had probably just come from their military term not long ago. At 32, Joe felt that he was too old for this. When the colonel entered the room, everyone rose. Joe remembered the guy from his first deployment as a corrupt and greedy colonel, who often came to his chubby daughter's apartment opposite Joe's at night to bring the spoils from the people who had bribed him.

"We are here today to once more serve our beloved Motherland," said the colonel rhetorically, "and no one is justified to refuse, decline, or give any pathetic reason, such as 'Oh, my wife is alone with three children and no help." No, sirs, you will report here in five days at the same hour, and you will receive your new uniforms," he shouted satisfactorily. He looked like he was expecting applause.

"Why 'don't you go instead, you stupid moron," mumbled Joe, and everyone nearby started giggling.

"Hey, ' 'what's going on over there? ' 'What's so funny? Oh, I see, ' 'It's the joker, his highness Corporal Joe. What a pleasure it is to have you among us! Well, this time, not even your cousin from the SS can save you ".

"My people from the workplace need me. They cannot find any replacement on such short notice. The whole factory will close, and they will lose a lot of export products. I thought the director made some arrangement with you?"

Oops, Joe meant to use the word 'discussion', but the 'morning's two glasses of cognac had sparked his arrogance and made it worse. He knew his boss had bribed the colonel with some goodies, and he should have kept his mouth shut. Everyone in the room knew what the word 'arrangement' meant.

The 'colonel's face changed from yellow to red, and he started shouting, "Nobody arranges anything with me! And 'you're going to be here on Monday morning at eight sharp, you hear me, soldier, because, for every minute late, you will get one day in prison! Class dismissed."

At that moment, he knew with certainty that he needed to escape. He must act and act quickly. He told his wife Alina what had happened and that he had decided to run away in a few days. She was reticent for a long time, but then unexpectedly, after a long pause, she said that her secretary had a brother who worked as a train conductor. His house was close to the border, and the train amazingly passed close by the Yugoslavian border.

Joe returned from his shocked trance and started listening. The conductor was a penniless guy, just married, who worked for the railway company and lived in a block apartment on a fourth level without a lift. He had to carry his 50-kilogram gas bottle up the stairs to the top level. All this he freely received from the Communist Party because of his good behaviour and hard work. The flat was very nicely painted directly over the concrete.

He was so poor that he slept with his wife and child on a small army bed and had just a table and two chairs.

Joe asked Alina to talk with her secretary about facilitating an urgent meeting with his brother.

Day 2

The next day, Joe contacted one of his mates who, for a long time, had wanted to buy his Fiat 850. Joe was heartbroken losing his 'baby', but the guy gave him the 30,000 Lei they had agreed on. Thanks to this little car, he had so many memories, such as travelling in the mountains with his wife and son and sometimes inviting his sister Tina and her two sons. But the highlight of his memories of the car was always after a soccer game, when he filled the car with his mates, taking seven people full of happiness and beer and driving to their homes.

Day 3

The meeting with the train conductor was the following day, around 9:00 a.m. The guy came to ' 'Joe's apartment and started admiring the rosewood library, the magnetophonon with Beatles music, the large TV with extra Yugoslavian channels (making four in total), and the large sofa. Joe told him about the forced enrolment in the army and that he needed to leave the country in two days. He said everything in the house would be given to him if he could take him and his brother-in-law to the border. The guy did not hesitate too long, and after the agreement, they shook hands and fixed a time and all other minor details, such as how to dress and act in front of the patrol soldiers on the train. They agreed that if the patrol asked, Joe and Vic would be his cousins who had come to his house (just 700 metres from the border) to help him process the pig.

Day 4

Joe did not go to work anymore because of his deployment. He let his boss know, thanked him for all the good times they'd had together, and sent many greetings to his colleagues. He called his sister and Vic in the morning, who had both taken a couple of days off work to discuss the upcoming event. Joe explained in detail what they needed to do, and because they both worked in a textile company, Joe asked them to make two black overcoats for the trip.

On the same day, Joe's first cousin, Michael from Moldova Nouă, visits him in Timisoara. Joe trusted Michael and told him about the enrolment and the plan to escape. Michael looked through the windows and saw two Serbs selling goods on the street.

"I have an idea. You also need to exchange some money, so come with me."

They went one level downstairs in the street and contacted the two Serbian guys. Michael, who knew their language better than Joe, explained the situation. For 20,000 Lei, they agreed to wait for Joe and Vic at the back of the town of Virbica, which was parallel to the Romanian village of Valcani from where they intended to cross.

At night, at about 10:00 p.m., the electricity went off as per the usual restriction. Joe lit two candles and studied the map again, and suddenly, he felt for the first time in his life that he needed divine intervention. He realised that no matter how much he memorised the map, nothing would happen as planned. In his emotional state, he started to pray: "Lord, if you help me cross the two borders and then get to Austria, I will be your follower forever."

Day 5

Joe did not sleep much that night. On D-Day, he started getting a massive migraine and began feeling anxious. Alina took the day off and prepared his little shoulder bag with water, preserved food, and a piece of smoked ham. Vic decided to go to the train station separately to meet Joe at 10:00 p.m.

Around 9:00 a.m., someone knocked on the door, and Joe opened it because Alina was outside at the market. He was shocked when he saw one of Alina's cousins, Pupu, sitting at the door. Joe had never had a close relationship with the guy; Pupu only visited him once as a student in the faculty of medicine. At that time, he needed some energy supplements and dry cacciatore salami from Joe. Thinking that he probably wanted to buy something, Joe invited him inside, and when the guy started talking about joining in the escape trip, Joe realised that it was a trap, and indeed, he was surely sent by security to catch him in action. Joe acted surprised and outraged, denying everything with so much passion that the guy left, somehow satisfied with the answer that nothing would happen.

After he went, Joe's anxiety grew even more extensive. "Someone is talking, but who?"

When Alina came home, Joe told her about Pupu's visit, and she was also shocked.

"He is the Security informer," she said.

She remembered that after he finished medicine at the university, Pupu had been dragged into a conspiracy with some generals looking to overthrow Ceaușescu. He had only played a small part in the mission, something to do with distributing a substance that would make the guards fall asleep. Unfortunately, the plot was discovered because one of the generals slept with a woman from high society and told her about the cup-the-tat. She was a snitch; as a result, all the generals were executed, and Pupu was tortured until he lost his mind. He had never worked as a doctor in his miserable life, but he'd discovered a new career as an informer.

Joe assured Alina that there was nothing to worry about, and they spent the afternoon dreaming of a new life and a new beginning in the springtime. She told him as a jock to apply for visas for all of them when he arrived in Austria.

At around 9:00 p.m., Joe embraced Alina for a last goodbye with feelings of fear in his heart, scared he would never see his family again.

"What happens is in the hand of God from now on," said Alina.

Joe took the bus and arrived at the train station around 9:40 p.m. Vic was already there. He got his bags, and they went into the toilets to change. They dressed in the overcoats on top of their clothes, added some small pillows to look fat, and closed their jackets.

"You look like an old fat butcher from the village nearby," said Vic, and they hopped up in the middle wagon.

The train started moving, and when they saw the conductor at the end of the wagon come over, the Traficant guy (called C) called them to go with him to the first passenger wagon where he could protect them.

Close to the border, the military patrol came to their compartment and asked for ID's. The soldiers knew C, and he explained that those people were with him and gave him 200 Lei. Not long after the soldiers left, the train arrived in Valcani village.

When they stepped out from the train, another checkpoint waited for them, and they queued in line. They were asked for their names and the address where they were going, but C intervened and explained they were his cousins who had come to help him kill the pig. When they were cleared to enter the village, walking down the road to his house, C told them they could not leave that night because they had been registered and must postpone until the next night.

At 11.30 p.m., they arrived at a very poor-looking house. When C knocked on the door, a middle-aged woman opened it and embraced C.

"Hey, guys, this is my mother," he said, and then both went into the kitchen to discuss the situation.

Suddenly, screaming came from the other room, and the woman shouted, "Do you want us to be imprisoned?"

Vic looked at Joe and blinked, saying: "Apparently, she pretended that she didn't know."

They heard the discussion, and C explained how much he would receive for his actions.

Then his mother shouted, "How about me? What do I get?"

She entered their room and asked them directly, "Do I get something from this?"

Vic asked her, "How much do you want?"

When she said 5,000 Lei, Joe looked at C, whose head was down. "This was not part of the deal, was it?" But he told the woman, "You will get 2,500 Lei tomorrow night when we depart." At that time, one US dollar was about 4 to 5 Lei in official trade at the bank. On the black market was like 1 US $ to 100 Lei. Paying a professional Traficant to help someone cross over in Serbia was 150,000 Lei.

She looked at C, who confirmed with his head that the boys could be trusted.

They went into a room with small beds and spent the night with all the images from their trip and all the worries of the future on their mind.

D Day

They woke up in the morning and sat in their room nearly all day because they couldn't be seen outside by any villagers who passed by. At around 11:00 p.m., Joe gave the woman the promised Money, who started crying and said she would pray for them.

C guided them through the backyard into the field, walking low, and after a few minutes, he said, That is as far as I can go."

Joe was furious. "But you promised us you would take us to the fence!"

C replied, "I'm terrified; I cannot go further, and it's only five hundred metres away. Good luck," he said and left.

So, Joe and Vic started crawling slowly to the fence.

Zagreb Station

With his head on the bus window, Joe looked at the beautiful city of Zagreb. The bus arrived and stopped in front of an impressive double-storey modern building.

"Let's go upstairs," said Joe.

They walked up to the second floor when suddenly a police patrol arrived to check people's IDs. They turned left to the lift, but another patrol came out.

"Let's go back down the stairs," said Joe.

They returned to the street, worried about what to do next, when Joe saw some taxis lined up.

"Let's take a cab and leave this dangerous area," said Joe.

They went to the first taxi in front, agreeing not to talk in Romanian. They entered the cab, and the old guy asked them where they wanted to go.

Joe said in English, "To Maribor customs border."

They left Zagreb station around 9:30 p.m. with immense relief.

The Hills

After 40 minutes of driving, Vic foolishly asked Joe in Romanian how far they had to go. Joe glanced at the driver, whose eyes were big. He looked scared. The guy tried to reach for his radio, but Joe stopped him by touching his hand. After a few kilometres, a light appears on the horizon. Joe asked the driver what this was. The old guy said that there were lights on the customs border.

Joe decided to stop a couple of kilometres before the border to avoid an incident. He asked the driver how much, and the guy said it cost 25,000 dinars. When Joe reached into his pocket for the Money, the driver retracted with a feeling of scared, thinking of some horrible idea. But when he saw the Money, he relaxed. Joe paid him around 40,000 dinars, which letter he regretted, and told him not to speak with anyone.

From there, they decided to travel on foot through the hills.

After a few hills, Vic was exhausted and said, "Look, no one is on the highway at this time; let's go back on the road."

Before they reached the road, a lovely memorial statue of Christ appeared in front of them. Joe was not a Christian, but he respected and understood spiritual things and remembered his grandparents reading the Bible to him when he was a little boy. Joe stopped a moment to meditate and thanked God they had travelled so far when he turns his head and saw Vic start urinating next to the obelisk.

Joe was outraged and his orthodox superstition starts to surface shouting at Vic: "You idiot ignorant, don't you have any respect? This is blasphemy; it could be bad luck for us."

"Sorry, I wasn't paying attention," replied Vic as an excuse.

They travelled along the road, ducking off the side of the road every time a car passed. They did this for half an hour but became more relaxed, which was when a police patrol spotted them on the side of the road. Two young police officers, about their age, got out of the car and asked them for IDs. Joe and Vic showed them their Romanian IDs because they did not have passports.

The leading officer investigated ID and exclaimed, "Aha, Romansky!"

Joe asked them in the English language, "Are you Serbs?"

The police guy replied, "No, we are Slovenian."

Joe said tremblingly, "Please, sir, you know what the Serbs will do to us if you send us back!"

They checked their bags, and when they saw only food and a map, they realised no drugs were involved. The officer looked at the other guy, lifted his shoulder, and said something about politics. He turned to the boys and motioned with the head towards the hills.

Joe and Vic did not wait for the other explanation and started running up the mountain, not even looking back, and expecting at any time to get a bullet in their back. When they stopped and looked down, the police car had disappeared.

Vic told Joe, "The taxi guy sold us out; luckily, these guys didn't want to work on the paperwork all night."

Joe said deeply and emotionally, "I believe those policemen were two angels who saved us."

They started the journey through the hills towards the border lights. There were about 11 small hills with steep inclinations of about 45 degrees.

"These hills are perfect for any army or football training," said Joe.

Each hill was challenging because their feet slipped on the leaves, and they were exhausted; they drank water that running downstream from the melting snow on that cold, wet February.

Joe fainted a couple of times, even though he was a fit guy. It was exhaustion, missed with fear equal a nightmare. When they reached the top of the hill, it was much easier to slide down on their back, wetting their clothes entirely. Joe took some clothing from the back of an open garden to dry his faces. Finally, they passed the east side of Maribor town and approached the international customs border.

Close to the end of their journey, Vic collapsed physically and mentally.

"It's payback for his act of insolence at the statue," criticises Joe in his mind. Vic was so skinny that Joe wondered how he'd made it that far. He tried to cheer him up, showing him that the border was not that far, but Vic refused to move on and said he would give up and surrender.

Joe tries extensively to negotiate. He left Vic and continue to push forward, travelled about one kilometre, but then his conscience told him this was wrong. His family would be disappointed with him for leaving Vic behind. He returned and found Vic in a much better physical form.

"What took you so long?" asked Vic.

"We've come so far, and I don't think I was right to abandon you," said Joe

He was glad that Vic had regained his strength, so they could continue this nightmare together, but he never told him.

They continued their journey and were on the last hill when they saw the sentinel tower on the left side.

"The real freedom is on the other side," said Vic.

The Second Borders

Down in the valley, the bright lights of customs showed six lines of trucks and cars ready to enter Leibnitz-Austria. It was about 6:10 a.m. when Joe looked at his father's watch.

"We are so late; daylight will be soon upon us," said Joe. "We need to run very fast. Can you, do it?"

Vic replied, "We've come so far, like the old say, it's now to the ballroom or to the hospital room."

They sprinted fast with their last breath, but the sentinel from the tower saw them and raised the alarm. Two huge lights started searching for them, and a very noisy alarm broke the silence of that morning. Everyone at the customs border stopped and wondered what was happening. They looked at the moving lights, which had not spotted the boys yet.

An extensive bunch of railway tracks appeared in front of them. Joe looked over his left shoulder and saw two shadows running toward them. The railway tracks protected the boys, and they reached the border before them. This time, even Joe saw the sand as they ran over it and left footprints. They continued running madly on the other side, probably not fully believing they were

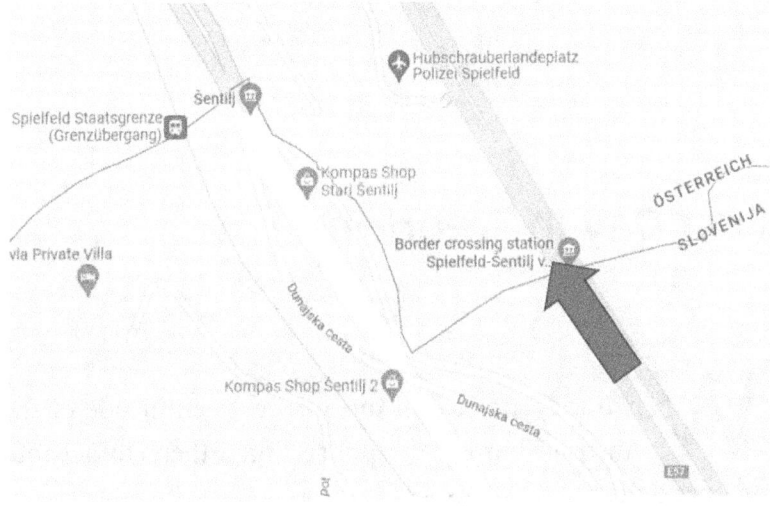

free in Austria. A jeep truck with a machine gun appeared from nowhere, and the Austrian soldier directed them towards the street in the valley, where police cars were waiting. One of the police guys threw his hat in the air. Everyone on the Austrian site of customs starts shouting with excitement. It was like live scenery from some movie, to see two people escape from the Iron Curtain from ruthless Serbian soldiers and enter Western society safe and sound.

First Day in Freedom

When they arrived on the Spielfeld-Sentilj side of the Austrian border, the police urged them to get into the cars quickly.

Joe showed them the yellow mud on their shoes, but the police guy said, "Don't worry, just get in."

So, the boys entered the brand-new Audi, which took them to the police station in Spielfeld.

When they arrived at the police station, a group of police, including two women and three men, came towards them with smiles, like they had achieved something in their monotonous job.

"it's a tremendous event. Nothing's happened around here for a long time; we are glad that you bring some excitement," said one of the policewomen, while everyone outside looked at the boys like they were from a zoo. They were asked a few questions, such as where they were from and how they'd got to this border. Both policemen exclaimed in admiration when they heard they were from Transylvania-Romania and had left 36 hours ago.

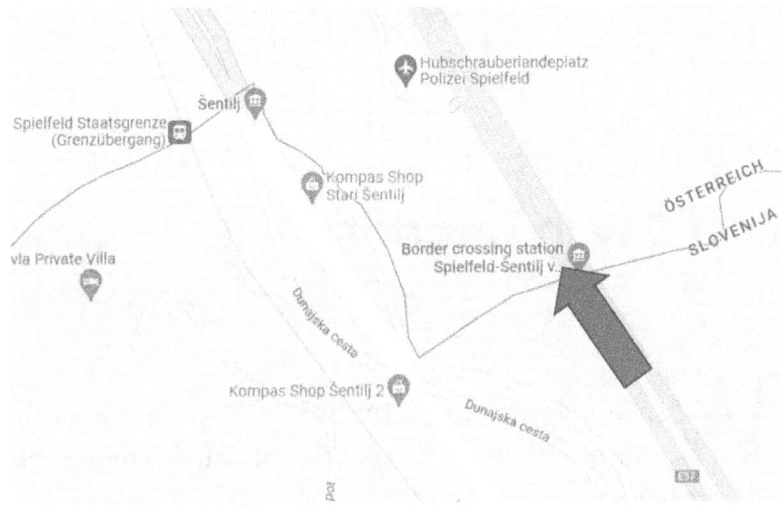

free in Austria. A jeep truck with a machine gun appeared from nowhere, and the Austrian soldier directed them towards the street in the valley, where police cars were waiting. One of the police guys threw his hat in the air. Everyone on the Austrian site of customs starts shouting with excitement. It was like live scenery from some movie, to see two people escape from the Iron Curtain from ruthless Serbian soldiers and enter Western society safe and sound.

First Day in Freedom

When they arrived on the Spielfeld-Sentilj side of the Austrian border, the police urged them to get into the cars quickly.

Joe showed them the yellow mud on their shoes, but the police guy said, "Don't worry, just get in."

So, the boys entered the brand-new Audi, which took them to the police station in Spielfeld.

When they arrived at the police station, a group of police, including two women and three men, came towards them with smiles, like they had achieved something in their monotonous job.

"it's a tremendous event. Nothing's happened around here for a long time; we are glad that you bring some excitement," said one of the policewomen, while everyone outside looked at the boys like they were from a zoo. They were asked a few questions, such as where they were from and how they'd got to this border. Both policemen exclaimed in admiration when they heard they were from Transylvania-Romania and had left 36 hours ago.

One asked them if they were hungry, and they confirmed by nodding. One of the guys asked them if they had any money, and when Joe showed them the Serbian dinars, everyone started laughing. When Joe showed them the 100 marks, they said, "Now we are talking."

The guy returned with two crusty bread sandwiches. Being on a stage of dehydration which made their mouths sensitive, the crust damaged their mouths and Joe started bleeding.

"Now we can see that you are telling us the truth; you are really from Transylvania," exclaimed one guy, and everyone started laughing.

They took the boys inside and let them clean themselves in the bathroom. The boys started washing their dirty faces and then cleaned the mud off their shoes. When they finished, they cleaned the room as they'd made quite a mess. One of the young police told them this would be recorded as good behaviour. Another policeman, who knew some geography, asked them which area they were born in and from where they crossed the borders.

When Joe replied, "Stayerdorfanina," another guy exclaimed, "Ooh, you came back!"

"No, silly," replied another guy. "This town is in Banat and was made by Frantz Joseph for extracting coal for the railways and tanks." Joe was very impressed by the history knowledge of the officer.

A superior policeman arrived, dispersing the group. He invited Joe and Vic into a room for interrogation. They needed to wait for an interpreter to come.

"They all are talking so nicely here, with the slow voice like they are reading a story," said Joe.

An older man, probably of retirement age, entered the room and introduced himself as George, the interpreter. He started asking many questions with a funny accent and a smiley face. He was good, paying attention to all the details the boys told him. For example, when he asked if they had joined the Communist Party, Joe said never, but Vic confirmed, which he regretted later.

After the interview, the interpreter told them that the rule for crossing the border was an offence and they needed to stay in a detention centre for two weeks, after which they would be released into the community and relocated to one of the Austrian towns. Then, one of the police officers from the border incident escorted the boys in a police car and drove them to the most prominent immigration camp: Transquirken. He took them to the register office wished them good luck, and left, very happy about his achievements.

"Even the police here are nicer and polite," commented Vic. From the office, they left with some documents to be registered from the camp's accommodation.

On the way to the second office, the boys agreed it was time to inform the girls about their incredibly successful escape. From one of the telephone boxes, Joe rang Alina at her mother's house. When she responded, he said, "Alina, it is me."

She started screaming with happiness, "Are you okay?"

"We are both good. Oh honey, it is so beautiful here in Austria. We are going to register for the detention camp now. Talk to you soon."

They talked for a few minutes and said farewell until the next time.

The boys waited in a long queue, so many people worldwide were registered voluntarily into the detention centre. They receive beds somewhere on level two in a building designed as a prison. When they entered a large room with 60 double beds, they did not like it very much, but they didn't have much choice. Joe remembered his army time and chose the top bed, hanging his little bag on the corner frame. Finally, both lay in bed and slept deeply for the first time in nearly 40 hours.

They were woken up in the evening by someone who spoke the Romanian language and told them it was dinnertime. So, they followed the group of people downstairs, waited in line to take their plates and plastic cutlery, and then walked in front of a stainless-steel food bench where the immigration cooks served them. They sat at the table and met other migrants from different countries from the communist bloc, like Poland or Czechoslovakia. Many Romanians in the room had formed a network, maybe because they were afraid or insecure and felt the need to protect each other from some inmates who escaped prison.

The two weeks passed; it was boring, and all they did was sleep and recover mentally and physically. The prison was not so challenging; they knew it would soon pass, and they would be free in the community. After two weeks, they were released outside to another building with a room, this time with only ten double beds. They were now free to go outside the camp and explore the little town.

The immigration had kindly put only Romanians in that room, and they soon made friends. They met two boys much younger than them, who attached themselves to Joe and Vic like they had known each other for a long time. They became good friends and started hanging out together, travelling to the village for window shopping. Some of the girls from the room followed them as well. They were all so happy, enjoying every moment, admiring the traditions and culture, and the design of the streets, houses and shops.

One day, Joe jumped on a bench in a beautiful central park, called everyone close to him, and said, "With this money, I bless you rich into this new world" He poured some Romanian currency onto their heads as it had no value in the West, and everyone started laughing.

They talked for a few minutes and said farewell until the next time.

The boys waited in a long queue, so many people worldwide were registered voluntarily into the detention centre. They receive beds somewhere on level two in a building designed as a prison. When they entered a large room with 60 double beds, they did not like it very much, but they didn't have much choice. Joe remembered his army time and chose the top bed, hanging his little bag on the corner frame. Finally, both lay in bed and slept deeply for the first time in nearly 40 hours.

They were woken up in the evening by someone who spoke the Romanian language and told them it was dinnertime. So, they followed the group of people downstairs, waited in line to take their plates and plastic cutlery, and then walked in front of a stainless-steel food bench where the immigration cooks served them. They sat at the table and met other migrants from different countries from the communist bloc, like Poland or Czechoslovakia. Many Romanians in the room had formed a network, maybe because they were afraid or insecure and felt the need to protect each other from some inmates who escaped prison.

The two weeks passed; it was boring, and all they did was sleep and recover mentally and physically. The prison was not so challenging; they knew it would soon pass, and they would be free in the community. After two weeks, they were released outside to another building with a room, this time with only ten double beds. They were now free to go outside the camp and explore the little town.

The immigration had kindly put only Romanians in that room, and they soon made friends. They met two boys much younger than them, who attached themselves to Joe and Vic like they had known each other for a long time. They became good friends and started hanging out together, travelling to the village for window shopping. Some of the girls from the room followed them as well. They were all so happy, enjoying every moment, admiring the traditions and culture, and the design of the streets, houses and shops.

One day, Joe jumped on a bench in a beautiful central park, called everyone close to him, and said, "With this money, I bless you rich into this new world" He poured some Romanian currency onto their heads as it had no value in the West, and everyone started laughing.

The Taste of Freedom

The next day, they were called to the front office for repartition. Joe asked the clerk if all four boys could be together in the same place.

She looked at them and said, "Okay, you guys, because you are all trade workers, I will send you to Linz, which is very far from here in the Oberosterreich region." She gave them the travel paperwork and told them to buy the tickets at the train station.

They jumped for joy and thanked the clerk for her kindness. The only inconvenience was that they had to travel separately. Joe and Vic received their travelling papers first, and the next day they walked to the train station and looked at the train that would take them to Linz. They had some time, so Joe rang Alina to let her know they were going to Linz.

They sat in the middle of the carriage, and when the train started moving, Joe felt an overwhelming euphoria that was hard to explain. It was like he had received a brand-new life.

The boys were impressed by everything from the smoothness of the train to the large windows, the view of the Danube and the castle, the perfection of the design and the cleanliness of the towns. It was like a picture from a dream about their endeavour for a second life.

Memories

With his head on the train window toward Linz, Joe meditated on his previous life. It had been pathetic, miserable, imperfect, full of mistakes, sins, lack of hope, depression, and alcohol abuse. "Why all that misery?" he asked himself. He turns to Vic and ask him: "Why we not been born in this society? look to this train is so clean and perfect, not even our pharmacies are that clean, and is so smoot, doesn't make any noise."

However, he was strongly determined to change, starting in the spring of 1989. He did blame the communist system for his miserable life, but he realised that part of it was because of his rebellious character and the lack of guidance in his life.

Joe was 11 years old when he lost his father, who died on the operation table from an overdose of anaesthetics that affected his heart. He only wants to remove the ulcer from his stomach that he inherited from his bitter day in the army as an officer. He meets Stasy, his wife, in a very dramatic event. Her sister Helen committed suicide because her boyfriend, a German guy from a Swab's clan, didn't want to marry her when he found out she was pregnant. She drowned in a lake, and the family called the military headquarters, where Joe's father was the commanding officer, to help retrieve the body from the lake with the scuba-diving soldiers.

After his death, his mother started having emotional rage because she'd lost her fairy-tale life and was forced to work harder, making life complicated and bitter for Joe and his sister.

At 18 years old, Joe finished high school with the Money he received from his father's military pension, and he left home, never to return. He attempted and passed all preliminary exams at the SS Military Academy but failed the medical examination because of his weak lungs. At 19, he started working as a quality controller at his first permanent job in a battery factory in Timisoara. After six months, he was drafted to compulsory enrolment in the army.

After completing two years in the army, Joe returned home to Timisoara. He struggled to find jobs, but a relative let him rent a room in the cellar for a minimal fee, where he survived without a heater when it was minus degrees outside. Joe got help from his mother's second husband, Handsy, who asked a favour from his boss to send Joe to a school of electricians in Arad, another Transylvanian town. Joe graduated and got a secure job in the construction industry. He became a hardworking character, learning skills from some old German Saxon colleagues.

In 1978, he married Alina and later had a son named Lucian. Unfortunately, both mothers didn't agree with this marriage, so Alina came up with the idea of telling her mother she was pregnant. In Romanian custom, the marriage must be initiated immediately.

At 23, the young couple rented an apartment till Joe transferred to a chemical company, where he received an apartment. After that, life was more favourable to them. Alina finished university with Joe's support and encouragement. She finally graduated as a chemical engineer. She was a genius girl, and in less than five years, she was promoted to a high rank in engineering in a company of more than 2000 people. Later, she was selected to work for a Canadian team to build a nuclear station outside Navodari on the Black Sea, another ambition of Ceaușescu uncontrollable madness.

Linz

When they arrived in Linz, they walked from the train station about five kilometres to the immigration camp. Joe saw a small church with large open doors and entered inside. It was the first church in which he sat and meditated. No one was in the chapel, and he got the courage to kneel in front of Jesus's cross and thank God for everything He'd done for them. But, first, he emptied himself of all the anxiety and stress by continuously crying. He felt a peace come over him like a lost child reunited with its parents after a long time.

> 'My chains are gone; I've been set free
> My God, my Saviour has ransomed me
> And like a flood, His mercy reigns
> Unending love
> Amazing grace.'

Not knowing how long he was inside, he left the church, but Vic understood and said nothing. They found a phone box and rang Alina at her mother's house. Having a telephone in the house was a luxury at that time. Joe informed Alina about Linz, the camp address, and promised to ring her more often. Alina told him something funny about the idiot colonel who had gone to his workplace to arrest him because of the five-day expiration. When he asked the workers where he was, they started laughing and one of the girls told him to look for Joe in Austria.

The boys went to the camp guided by local people, and after walking down a long alley, they saw two large apartment blocks with five levels and another four blocks with two levels. They went to the main office and handed in their transition papers. After registration and a short interview, the camp manager, called "Bitte," gave them a key and assigned them to block four, level one, in a nice cosy room. Unfortunately, they had to share a toilet with everyone on the same floor.

"Let's get the toiletry products before the store closes today," said Joe.

So, they went downstairs to a storeroom and received some toiletry items from a lovely lady who welcomed them in German, tickets for the canteen and 40 shillings each for one week. Information on the opening and closing times of the store was on the back of their tickets.

They found out from the large size security officer, baptised with the nickname 'Hop-a-la'. He was posted in a nice kiosk just behind the entrance and told them the camp was open at 6:00 a.m. and closed at 10:00 p.m. The guy comes outside from his cabin, barely makes it from the door, and starts talking in English with the boys. He gave them a lot of information, advising them not to associate with Albanians from the other block. "Hazardous people," he said, "and many of them will be sent back to their country. Do not take the kindness of Bitte for granted because even though he is very kind and generous, he's a tough guy for such a small person." He started laughing. "He sent hundreds of people home, so be very careful," he added.

The boys explored the camp and visited the canteen with a large kitchen, all in modern stainless steel. It was a massive room with probably 20 big tables and two serving desks, behind which several cooks and chefs worked to prepare the meals. Outside was a large area divided into a playground and a small soccer field, which pleased Joe incredibly. In the middle of the camp was a small building, and they discovered it was a medical building with one doctor and a few nurses. It was all designed to be the most convenient accommodation; free beds, free food, and pocket money to enjoy the best holiday they'd ever have.

They saw people running towards the canteen and asked them why. Someone said something about not missing the limited bratwurst sausage. So they went inside and waited in the queue with their plates and were pleased to see four or five variations of food that looked so beautiful. It was like magic when they sat at the table and tested the food.

"It is always like this?" asked Vic of the guy beside him.

"O ye, even better," said the young guy.

They didn't have a meal like this for a very long time.

They went upstairs towards their room and, passing by the corridor, observed that some rooms had TVs inside, and they wondered how this was possible. So they returned to the fat security guy and asked about a TV. He started laughing and said that the management closed their eyes to what people had in their rooms as long as they were not stolen products.

"Those TVs you see are from town people who throw their trash in the front house for collection. If you find something in good condition, you can have it. People have everything here in the camp, from bicycles to cars. Bitte closes his eyes if some people are working and whether they pay or not for their rent. Yaa, yaa, if their comportment is good, then it is no problem. We encourage people to be active in working and not stealing. Look at the car outside; not even our staff have cars like this. It is what the Americans are saying—the land of opportunity. They can sit here until they receive a visa from America, Canada, or Australia."

The boys left with a sense of awe and excitement that was hard to express. The whole world had opened to them, and they couldn't wait to see what opportunities arose.

"First, we need transport—we need a bicycle—and then we need to find jobs," said Joe.

They found a few people in the hall downstairs that were Romanian. They had lots of information about life in the camp and town. All admin staff left the centre at 5:00 p.m., and only the cooks remained till 7:00 p.m. The guards were 24/7, some very strict, and they all had guns.

They were allowed to purchase drinks from the cabinet machine, such as Coca-Cola and beer. But because it was their first day, one guy offered a beer to them. Joe gave the beer to Vic, and the same guy said, "Don't worry, I'll get you another one." He pulled a small wire from his jacket and pushed the wire inside the vending machine through the coin slot. Finally, after a few attempts, a beer came out of the collection hole. "See, everything is free in this country!"

The following day after breakfast, the boys hunted for a bicycle. They borrowed a universal spanner and started walking on the streets of Linz. After a few hours, they finally found a bike through the trunk in front of an apartment block. It had a flat tyre, so they carried it to the camp and started fixing it.

Back in the camp, one guy with an Arabian accent told them that there was a place outside the town where all the bicycles were piled up, and a good Samaritan repaired them for free. He offered to drive them to that place, and they gladly accepted. When they arrive, a fantastic scenery of a massive stockpile of all sorts of bicycles appears. They were grateful to the driver, who also gave them some of his tools, and Joe promised to return them at the camp. They spent a couple of hours there and managed to assemble two bicycles that looked like new.

"I can't believe we have transportation in the first 24 hours since we've come to Linz," said Joe.

They returned to the camp just in time for lunch and admired the buildings in the town on their way back, with so many different colours, the cleanliness of the paved streets, and the variety of shops with large windows that showed all the products inside. They had never felt so alive and full of joy.

The Camp

Life in the camp in the first month was like in a holiday resort. They had secure transportation, but the more they saw people prosper in the centre, the more they desired to have more for themselves. Joe dreamt of having a car. Vic did not care much about this because he had no driver's licence but wanted to travel.

Unfortunately, they discovered that most people acquired goods by stealing, forming gangs of four or five people and taking from expensive shops. One distracted the salesman, and the other hid the products under their clothing. Afterwards, they cut the electronic tag off, jumped quickly into the waiting car outside, and vanished.

One day, a guy knocked on their door, asking them if they wanted to buy a leather XL jacket.

Vic politely refused and said, "We just come here and don't have any money," which was true because they had to survive on 40 shillings per week.

"Oh, I understand, but you can pay me later. You can work on the black market to make Money if you want to work. A friend of mine is a construction supervisor, and he needs people for different jobs." He told them the man's name and where to find him.

They found the guy and were offered a deal to work eight hours for 100 Shillings cash, but only two days per week. Joe accepted, and after another month, their lives improved dramatically. They changed their wardrobe, found a good TV from the streets where they had been working and started to get acquainted with all the supermarkets close to the camp. A highlight was window shopping in a large shopping centre, which they had never seen before.

"If only they were here with us," said Joe melancholically, thinking about his wife. They missed their family because only when they were together would their life feel complete.

They went to the office to get an audience with 'Bitte' the manager and asked him many questions about their alternatives. The guy was honest and told them everything they wanted to know. It was an ugly truth. They could not depart from any country as individual asylum seekers if they did not have an entire family in the camp. Singles had to wait a very long time for their drafts, sometimes up to two years. However, after reuniting with the family, the departure process to another country would take a maximum of six months. They left the office disappointed and heartbroken, with no hopes for the future.

Joe jumped on the bicycle to clear his mind and rode through the towns, and then something inside drew him to the first little church he'd visited there. He entered and began to pray to God to give him an answer, hope, or anything to hang on to.

When he returned to the camp, Vic said, "We need to let them know. We need to let Alina and Tina know about this situation."

Joe was angry. "And what do you want me to tell them, that all this was for nothing and that we will be separated for years?"

However, they did ring and tell the girls the misfortunate information. It was a sorrowful day for everyone. The world seemed to have collapsed around them, their happiness had disappeared in the wind, and nothing made sense anymore. There was no way that they could bring the girls on an official government application. The reunification would only happen after years of waiting.

But life continued, and the boys worked hard to occupy their time. Something inside told them to keep hoping, to be patient and wait. They shared the job with their two friends from the Transquirken camp, who had arrived the day after them and had not found work.

All four boys formed a strong friendship, and everyone from the camp started to envy and respect them. They were all tall boys of between 1.85 to 1.90 centimetres. One day, a guy started making horrible jokes, cursing and swearing when a small Christian group offered to sing some of their songs in the corridor inside the building.

Like many anxious people who felt bitter about life and influenced by the latest bad news, Joe listened to the songs, needing spirituality and peace for his troubled heart. But this guy continuously started cursing and swearing at the group to leave and bully everyone. Joe had enough of this insolence, and intervened by pushing the guy, who tried to swing a punch at him. Joe ducked and pushed the guy -maybe a bit hard- into his door, which broke from its hinges. There was a moment of silence, and Joe lifted his shoulders and hands and said, "Sorry, I could not help it." Then the music started again. No one made any comment, maybe because they were used to the Romanian custom and tradition, or simply no one cared.

One morning, someone knocked on the door and told the boys a woman wanted to talk to them on the phone. Joe went to the corridor phone and spoke to Alina, who asked him to come to Spielfeld to pick them up because they had also escaped to Austria. Joe, not fully awake, could not comprehend at first the gravity of the situation and the importance of the event. He asked questions, and Alina repeated herself till she lost patience and started screaming at Joe to come there at once. She gave him the address of a petrol station, just a few metres from the border.

When they finished their conversation, Joe told Vic the big news. They both were paralysed with disbelief. Joe was amazed at how God had listened to his prayers and sped up the process in life.

Joe needed a car, but as no one wanted to lend a car for one day, he had to buy one. He found an old bomb of a car for which the boys negotiated a price of 500 shillings. He was not legally allowed to leave Linz, but he didn't care. He was so anxious to bring his wife to him and a safe place. So, he filled the car with cheap petrol and started driving on the Autobahn at 120 km/hour, watching the new cars pass by at 180-200 km/hour.

After four hours of driving on the Autobahn, he finally arrived in Spielfeld near the international border separating Eastern Europe from Western Europe. He felt a sensation of heat in his body and heavy sweat on his forehead because the Iron Curtain was now so close by. He went to the petrol station where he was supposed to pick up the girls, parked the car, and waited an hour. Finally, he could no longer wait and decided to leave. Any police car could spot the rusty Nissan with Linz number plates, and he could be in trouble because he'd left the camp. Migrants were not allowed mobile phones, so they could not communicate in any way.

He went back to Linz and waited for the girls to call. When they called in the evening, Joe asked them what had happened and why they weren't waiting for him. Alina told him they had waited too long, and then they had been afraid and returned to the hotel where a lovely manager woman took care of them. They fixed another meeting for the next day, but this time Joe asked for the hotel address and a phone number just in case and was told that the trip would take about four hours, and only if the old car could do it again. From then on, they all learned that proper communication was essential in their life in Western society!

When Joe arrived at the hotel, the girls were outside waiting. There was another girl with them, and they explained the entire story on the road. She wanted to escape because of her Canadian boyfriend, who promised to marry her. Later, she found out he was already engaged in Canada.

Joe decided that he would not report the girls to Transquirken immigration. He drove to Linz to show the girls around and have fun together. They told him how they crossed the borders, and Joe was amazed by their story.

Alina story about her decision to escape comes after she realise what Joe says on that day at the phone, that the immigration is approved visa only for integrated family. She was sick by been molested by colleagues at work, she lost the government apartment, and even her own family were against about such a dangerous action. Somehow, by miracle, she found that girl Eva, who promised that her relative will help them to cross Yugoslavia. They also agree to take Tina with them.

On the night of 15 of Aprill, on the first border, the same guy "C" who'd helped Joe and Vic, guided the girls help (for a reasonable price) but this time right to the fence at the border. He cut the fence and help the girls slide under the rocket wire. When they crossed the channel, they made so much noise that probably even the dogs from the nearby village could heard them.

Then another miracle, they find Eva relative waiting for them on the other site of the village, which was another exciting part of the story. On that night the girls start crossing, her cousin and his wife from Australia already waited for them near the highway on the other side of the village. Miraculously, the girls were guided by a strange force directly to the meeting point with the cousin and his wife. They were shocked by disbelief and happiness and calculated the probability of this event as one in 1000 because of the large border area.

When they saw the girls, the woman exclaimed, "Oh my God, it is a miracle." They drove the wet girls in a rented Mercedes to their relatives' house in Novi Sad, a large town in Banat, Serbia. They helped the girls clean up and gave them food and dry clothing. The girls told of their adventure crossing the border.

The following day, they drove to the Maribor border. Here, the guy gave the girls two options: to cross the border on the railway tracks or go via the hills. Naturally, the girls chose the railway, which was more accessible but much more dangerous because soldiers heavily protected it.

The night came much earlier in Aprill, and the girls started walking on the railway trucks around 8:00 p.m. They had no idea the sentinels were changing their shift as the sentinel had already left and did not wait for the replacement guard. And so, they kept walking like in the fairy tell movie and even heard the soldiers showering in the posthouse. They continue walked until Tina got tired and fell into a pit beside the railway because she wasn't looking where she was going. Then the other two girls heard the noise, they turned, and looked for Tina who had disappeared. It was a funny moment on their journey, but there was no time to laugh, so they just push on going.

Not much further, they saw some colourful lights, and when they saw a small road, they used a block of concrete to slide down from the railway.

From there, they followed the little street to the highway. The petrol station was owned by Agip, represented by the six-legged yellow Woolf sign showing them they were definitely in Austria. The hotel nearby attracted them with its warm lights inside. It was closed, but they saw a woman working inside and knocked on the door.

When the woman opened the door, she saw three girls sitting in front of the door, looking miserable and exhausted. They told their story in English language about how they crossed the border and how they arrived at this motel. The woman was amazed at their courage, and she tried to explain in her poor English language that a day before, the Serbs had shot six people who attempted to escape. From the hotel, they rang Joe and waited for him to come and rescue them. However, they did not want to surrender to the police because they feared being sent back to Yugoslavia.

A New Beginning in Springtime

In May 1989, Joe and the girls arrived in Linz. He smuggled the girls inside the building and into their room. It was an exciting reunion moment, and everyone cried with happiness. It was a miracle, and Joe said God had listened to their prayers. They called their other two friends and celebrated with beer from the vending machine.

The next day, Joe took the girls to the Transquirken camp for registration. The girls make the mistake of telling the immigration guy that Joe has brought them to the base, and the guy thinks that Joe has helped them to cross the border. The immigration office called Joe to "please explain", and he clarified that he had only picked up the girls from the Sentily gas station in Spielfeld and had nothing to do with them crossing the border.

Sitting at the back of the room, the senior commanding officer said, "This is an amazing story, something unheard of. Three girls make fools of the ferocious and unmerciful Serbian soldiers, crossing the border alone, without any guide. This case has happened for the first time in our border history."

Joe was dismissed, and he returned to Linz and told everyone the girls' story.

Encouraged by this story, a lovely Christian Romanian guy convinced his wife to escape along the same route. Together with two other girls and three boys, they attempted to cross the border at the same place, but the Serbians caught all of them except for one boy. They kept the girls a bit longer for pleasure, then imprisoned them. Later, they released the girls, thanks to UNICEF in Vienna, and they came to Austria.

The wife of the Romanian Christian man became pregnant through this awful experience. All the people in the camp treated them with empathy and compassion.

After two weeks, Joe and Vic received their wives in Linz, released from the Transquirken camp. After one month, the camp management moved both families to a block with only two-level apartments. The rooms had two bunk beds and a small bathroom with a toilet and a miniature shower inside. Everything was just perfect.

The Working Class

Both families put in three applications for asylum, first to the USA, then Canada, and last to Australia, and waited for the first Embassy to respond. In the meantime, they enjoyed their lives, riding their bicycles along the Danube River, walking in fancy parks, visiting the museums, and everything that did not involve Money.

"We need to find jobs," said Joe. "We should ask those with jobs if their bosses need extra hands."

The idea worked; Tina took over a job from a friend who left for Canada, cleaning in the morning at a restaurant in the city. Vic found a job as a handyman at a veteran estate, and Alina found a job at the fish factory. A few weeks later, Joe received a government yellow card, which meant he could work officially everywhere he wanted. Only a few of the entire 2000 people in the camp have this opportunity of such a card. Joe went to the workforce office and received a fax printed with five electrical jobs from different companies in the town. At the first company, the owner asks Joe if he can speak German to communicate as the other workers don't understand English.

Joe tried the second company but received the same answer. However, the third time, he struck luckily. The owner, an old guy, interviewed him in English, found out that Joe had a grade five in electricity, and told him that he would be put on trial. The company was Smith & Packler, Industrial and Commercial Electrical Services.

Joe started working the next day with a broadband cable unit. His supervisor was a 63-year-old guy, close to retirement age. They aimed to dig a small channel in a particular area for broadband cable. The procedure was to dig 10 metres until they reached a beer case. Then, they were to take a *'spritz pausen'* by drinking a beer each and continue to the next one. One week of working passed quickly, and Joe never missed a day because of the incentives. One day a supervisor came to the workplace and told Joe he had another mission.

"I haven't finished here; I can't leave the old guy to dig by himself," Joe tried to explain.

"Don't worry; another team will start this job today," said the supervisor, Fritz.

He took Joe in a company van, drove toward the city and stopped in front of a block with four levels where Joe had to fix an issue with the electric board. He looked at Fritz, who smiled, delighted with the work. After another two weeks, Joe was sent to the primary team or the master's team. There were six in the group including the supervisor. They had their own van, store, and permanent contract work providing electrical jobs and service to the new paper company, Nachtscriten.

The money he received from the job was a dream come true and helped add more comfort to their lifestyle. The food and camp accommodation were free, and Bitte didn't mind if they worked because he thought it was better to work than to steal.

Alina also finds a job in a fish factory, Tina in a restaurant and Vic in private maintenance. After the first working month, Joe bought, with 5,000 shillings, a beautiful light blue Honda Acord with a blue velvet interior. He registered the car, and every weekend the family went on trips around Oberosterreich in northwest Austria. The highlights were the town and the castle of Salzburg and visiting the horrible. Mauthausen camp.

Visa

Time flew past, and after nearly a year, they received news from the Australian Embassy that they had been drafted for asylum in Australia. Vic and the girls were so excited, but Joe, who had just received Austrian black passports with the silver eagle for him and Alina, wasn't happy with this outcome. He loved Austria, he loved to travel in Europe, and he loved his job. So, when the Austrian Government invited Joe and Alina to remain in Austria, Joe was excited. The guy interviewing Joe and Alina said that not many people receive those passports in such a short time. Joe tried to be funny and said this is a phenomenon legacy from his grandad who was in the First War in the Austro-Hungary army.

However, Alina refused the deal, arguing the idea of remaining in Austria. "We crossed the border, risked our lives to escape together, and now you want us to be separated." She refuses a further offer from the Government of a job as an engineer in one of the largest crane factories in Linz and two years of training in commercial selling around Europe. Something unthinkable! They also offered three apartments to choose from around Linz and 70,000 shillings to start their life. However, she refused all those offers, which she regretted later on in her life.

Because of this situation, there was a lot of tension between Joe and his wife.

One more thing they needed to do was to bring Lucian from behind the Iron Curtain to Linz. Other Romanians from the camp advised them that the only solution was to apply at the magistrate's court in Linz. Two months later, Lucian came to Linz. As a minor, he was accompanied on the plane from Timisoara to Viena by a Romanian steward who told him, "Is this country not good enough for you?"

Another miracle had happened.

They were now all reunited, Tina and Vic's kids as well. Together, they enjoyed travelling every weekend in Joe's car, wherever they wanted. On one of the long weekends, Joe and Alina planned to go to Italy. But unfortunately, they were called to Vienna by the Australian Embassy and told to surrender their Austrian passports and complete all the paperwork because they would depart soon. Alina and Tina were overwhelmed by the news.

They were invited inside the Ambassador's office for the meeting. The Ambassador made a joke about Ceaușescu and started laughing hysterically. They did not understand his joke, so they only smiled politely, which made the Ambassador suspicious, and think they were probably still under the curse of the communist influence. Finally, he gave them their documents and told them to wait at the camp while the Embassy organised their transportation for departure to Australia.

Vic, Tina and their kids were the first to leave, and they arrived in Melbourne. The cousins from Melbourne, Nick and Cicci with their wives, and many from the Romanian community received them enthusiastically.

Joe and Alina could not depart because they had just had a beautiful baby girl and had to postpone until she was three months old and could have a picture in the basket added to the travel documents. Their waiting time in Linz was a bit sad. Lucian attempted the fifth grade and had some issues with the other kids, being considered 'Auslander'- meaning an outsider even though he had more blond hair and green eyes than anyone. Alina was busy with Anna, and Joe had retired from his job, feeling sad and uncertain about the future. However, he received some presents from the company and a lovely letter of recommendation for his future employment.

Joe felt depressed about losing his excellent job and leaving his lovely colleagues, mates, and this wonderful country. He remembered how they finished work at noon every Friday, and all had lunch on the restaurant terrace, paid for by the company. He had a beautiful life, but it now seemed lost. They could be such wealthy people if they remained in Austria. Joe's excellent job had made him a fortune, and he'd become involved with a group of Pentecostals selling cars in Romania, from which he took a percentage. With his Austrian passport, he could buy cars from Linz car yards and sell them in Romania at a double price because of the high demand for vehicles there. In one year, they built a church in Transylvania with this Money that cost US $800,000. At the time, he'd thought he would remain in Austria and did not anticipate needing that money for the next step on his journey and spending it all unwisely.

The day of departure arrived, and an official escorted them to the departure gate of Olympus Airline in Vienna. They arrived in Athens in the evening and were accommodated at the hotel next to the airport. They saw the city in the evening, and Joe immersed Anna in the Aegean Sea as a symbol of baptism.

Australia

The next day they departed with the same Olympus Airline, and all four arrived in Melbourne on March 21, 1990, the same day Joe had escaped from Romania. The large group of people who waited for Vic and his family were in the waiting area to cheer up Joe's family. In time, Joe and Alina realised that those people were relatives of the Romanian Baptist Church. When a woman from immigration services asked Joe if they had a place to stay, Cicci, his cousin, said, "They will stay with us."

And so, they started a new chapter in their life in the country at the end of the world. Joe and Vic's family joined their cousin in the First Romanian Baptist community church from Richmond. A few months later, they were baptised and became followers of Christ.

They all started working. Joe's electrician's license was not recognised, so he became a truck driver like all his cousins. Four years later, in 1994, they built their first house on their land.

"We own a piece of this earth," said Alina to Joe.

It was hard to start everything from scratch. Initially, they struggled to survive, asking themselves, like Hebrew people escaping from

Egypt, why they were here. Money was never enough. Still, because a carrying God cared for everything in time, they finally understood why they were here at the earth's end.

The kids loved their school, they had their first dog, and they never lacked food on their table. Joe and Alina were very proud when their son achieved a degree at Monash University and their daughter had a degree as a graphic designer.

The family enjoyed the freedom of travelling by seeing every corner of the country and never ceased to be amazed by the beauty of Australian nature. Joe and Alina served for 33 years in the Christian community. Joe continued to love the scripture and was encouraged by the senior pastor John from a large church in Adelaide to complete a Bachelor of Ministry. He loves working in the missionary field, and his vision of going to Ukraine as a missionary and making a difference in this chaotic world, would be like a dream come true.

Nothing had made sense in their life before they came to Australia. They now had freedom, a purpose in life, hope, health, joy, and happiness.

Think big and dream big! All that is needed is to have faith in God. He will never leave or forsake his people with genuine faith.

Joe compared his life to a caterpillar. Before transforming into a butterfly, had an ugly life, but after the transformation, spread its wings, and flew away freely.

The absolute freedom they experienced was not by crossing two borders into the Western society, but the understanding the real meaning of life.

Joe now saw the world with different eyes, understanding people as they were, with their differences, struggles and joys. He observed the wonder of Mother Nature, the beautiful forests, and the creek estuary that fed into the ocean with olive colour and white waves. The great escape had not only from a communist country but from himself. All this had become possible only when he felt the absolute peace of God in his heart.

> "The Lord has promised good to me
> His word, my hope, secures
> He will my shield and portion be
> As long as life endures."

Commentary

Dear Joseph,

Thanks for sending in your work to us on this extraordinary story of escape from behind the Iron Curtain.

There was plenty of tension and suspense throughout the storyline with the series of events that take place to finally get the main characters to safety in Linz, and then their wives afterwards. You provide an excellent insight into the fear that people had during these particular events and the difficulties they faced getting to safety.

There were some excellent descriptions from the scary moments in the mud by the border to meeting Austrian police and wondering what they might do, entering the camp, and driving across the country to bring their wives to safety.

The reader feels transported along with Joe and Vic, and will no doubt feel some of the same emotions. Along with these varied emotions, there is good use of dialogue and narrative to tell the story. I assume you could be the Joe in the story and thank you for sharing it with others. I'm sure many people will be touched by these events and come to understand the difficulties many in the communist bloc faced.

All the best with this story and I wish you every success with it.

Kind regards,
Joane - Editor www.FirstEditing.com

www.ingramcontent.com/pod-product-compliance
Lightning Source LLC
Chambersburg PA
CBHW071848290426
44109CB00017B/1977